Acknowledgements

Educational consultant Viv Edwards,
Professor of Language in Education, University of Reading.
Illustrations by Steve Cox.
Photographs by Zul Mukhida except for:
p.3b Paul Harmer; pp.4l,4r,5 Tim Garrod, pp.7,8 John Heinrich,
pp.9t,9b Doug Green, p.10l Graham Horner, p.10m John Heinrich,
p.11r Tim Garrod, p.11l John Heinrich, pp.12,13t,13b Tim Garrod,
p.14t Doug Green, p.16b Graham Horner, pp.17,18l John Heinrich,
p.19 Doug Green, back cover (left) John Heinrich, Zul Colour Library;
p.14b Paul Harmer; p.15 Mike Guy, V.K. Guy Limited.

The author and publisher would like to thank the staff and
pupils of Balfour Infant School, Brighton and Somerhill Junior
School, Hove; Simon Hart; Paul Carter, Brighton & Hove Bus
and Coach Co. Ltd; Annmarie and Adrian Yeeles.

A CIP catalogue record for this book is available
from the British Library.

ISBN 0-7136-4031-6

First published 1994 by A & C Black (Publishers) Ltd
35 Bedford Row, London WC1R 4JH

© 1994 A & C Black (Publishers) Ltd

Typeset in 15/21pt Univers Medium by
Rowland Phototypesetting Ltd, Bury St Edmunds, Suffolk.
Printed in Belgium by Proost International Book Production

Transport

Nicola Edwards

A&C Black · London

Cars, trains, ships and planes often have messages on them. Sometimes the message is an advertisement.

Sometimes the message can help you with your journey.

The list in the window of this train tells the passengers where the train will be stopping.

Look at the cars in this photograph. Which one is the taxi? How can you tell?

A bus has a number on it to show you which way it is going.

These people are waiting at a bus stop. The numbers on the sign tell people which buses will stop there.

When a bus arrives at the bus stop, people look at the number on the front of the bus. Next to the number is the name of the place where the bus will finish its journey.

Cars often have signs on them.

At the front and back of every car there is a number plate, which can tell you about the car.

The letter G at the start of this British number plate tells you that the car was new in 1989.

The letters HH at the start of this German number plate tell you that the driver of the car lives in Hamburg.

The letter L on this sign tells you that the driver of this car is learning to drive.

When people drive their car abroad, they put a sticker on the back of the car to show which country they come from.

Which countries do you think the people driving these cars have come from?

There are messages inside cars, too.

This dial tells the driver
how fast the car is moving.

This sign tells the
driver how much
fuel is in the tank.

This light comes on to warn the
driver that the car's engine
is running out of oil.

What other signs can you see?
Can you find out what they are for?

These pictures were taken inside an aeroplane.

How many different messages can you see?
What do the messages tell you?

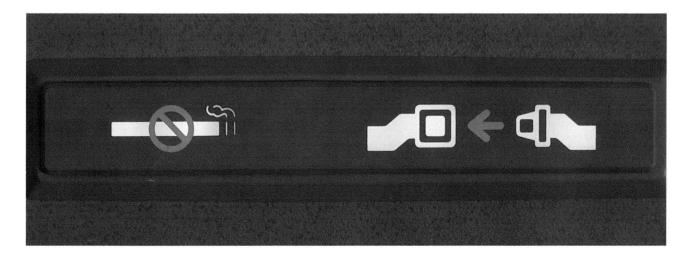

Messages on signposts can help people with their journeys. Signposts

. . . give directions

. . . give information

. . . warn drivers of danger.

What messages do you think the signposts are giving in these pictures?

Markings on roads can give messages, too.

The black and white stripes on this road show people where they can cross the road safely. Why do you think this is called a zebra crossing?

What do you think the markings mean on this road?

Lights can tell you when to stop and when to go.

The flow of traffic at this crossing is controlled by lights.

The red light tells drivers they must stop. The green light tells people on foot that they can cross the road.

The amber light flashes to tell drivers that they can go forward if no-one is still crossing the road.

The green light flashes to warn people on the crossing that the traffic is about to start moving again.

This green light tells drivers it is time to move off.
The red light warns people on foot not to cross the road.

Lights can also show the way.

The lights on this runway show pilots where to land their aeroplanes.

The lights on cars light the road ahead when it is dark. Street lights also help drivers to see where they are going.

The flashing light on top of this lighthouse warns passing ships and boats that there are dangerous rocks nearby.

Sounds can give messages to people making journeys.

The guard on this station platform blows a whistle to show that the train is about to leave.

The siren on this fire engine makes a loud noise. The noise warns other drivers to let the fire engine pass.

Do you have a bicycle with a bell on it?
What do you use the bell for?

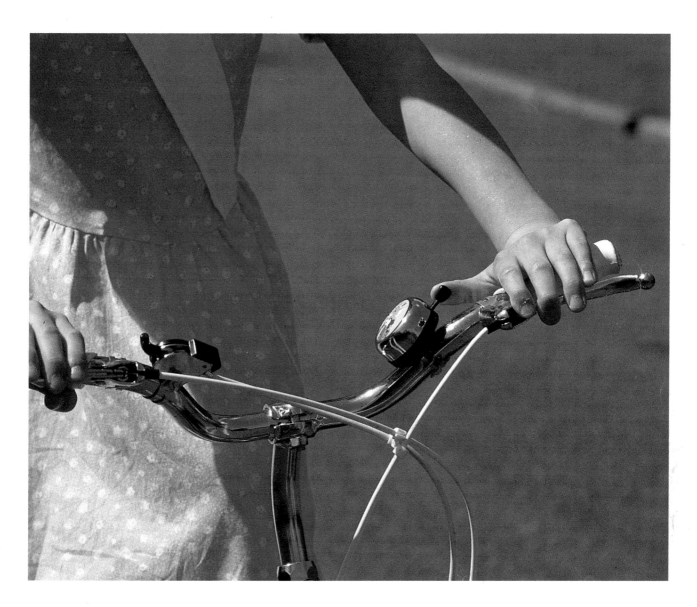

People use their arms to signal to others.

This policeman is using arm signals to direct the traffic.

This cyclist puts her arm out to show that she wants to turn right.

This airport worker is signalling to show
the pilot where to bring the plane to a stop.

When you travel by train or bus, a timetable
can help you to plan your journey.

This is part of a bus timetable. Which bus
would you catch from Beckford to arrive
at Maze End by half past ten?

Which bus would you catch from Park Road
to get to Chalk Lane at eleven o'clock?

Nº4 Bus route — Beckford to Maze End

Mondays to Fridays							
Beckford	8·00	8·30	9·00	9·30	10·00	10·30	11·00
High Street	8·10	8·40	9·10	9·40	10·10	10·40	11·10
Park Road	8·15	8·45	9·15	9·45	10·15	10·45	11·15
Bridge Street	8·25	8·55	9·25	9·55	10·25	10·55	11·25
Chalk Lane	8·30	9·00	9·30	10·00	10·30	11·00	11·30
Sandy Way	8·40	9·10	9·40	10·10	10·40	11·10	11·40
Long Lane	8·45	9·15	9·45	10·15	10·45	11·15	11·45
Meadow Road	8·55	9·25	9·55	10·25	10·55	11·25	11·55
Maze End	9·00	9·30	10·00	10·30	11·00	11·30	12·00
Mondays to Fridays - continued							

When you travel on a bus, ship, train or aeroplane, you need a ticket to show that you have paid for the journey.

This boy is showing his ticket to the ticket inspector before he gets on the train.

A ticket can show:

the date and the time that you bought the ticket

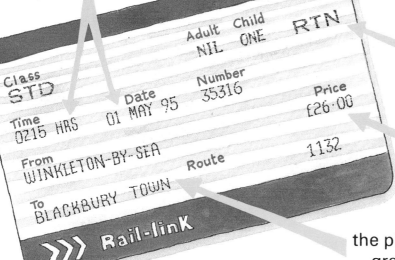

whether it is for a single or return journey

how much you paid for it

the place where you are travelling to

Adult Child RTN
NIL ONE

Class
STD

Date
01 MAY 95

Number
35316

Price
£26·00

Time
0215 HRS

From
WINKLETON-BY-SEA

Route
1132

To
BLACKBURY TOWN

>>> Rail-link

A map can help you to find your way from one place to another.

Here is a map of a village.

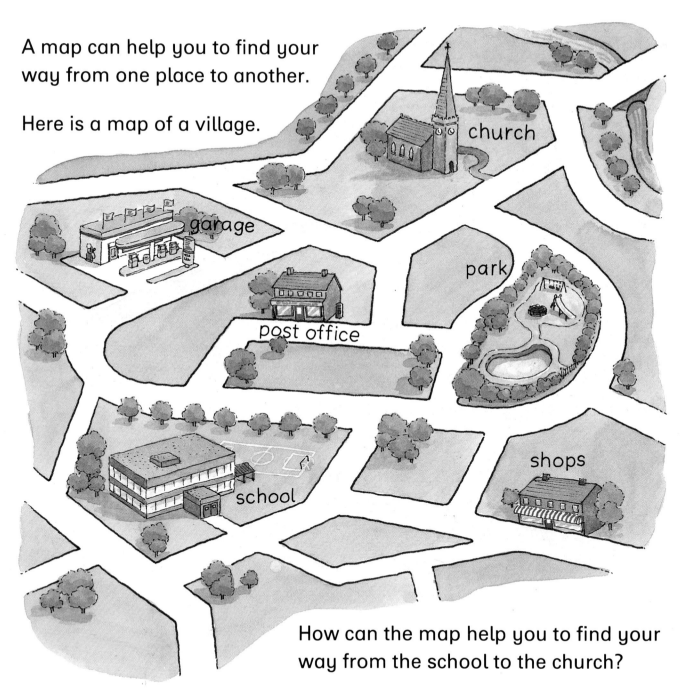

How can the map help you to find your way from the school to the church?

Maps can be different shapes and sizes.
How many can you see in this picture?

Index

For parents and teachers

The aim of the *Messages* series is to help build confidence in children who are just beginning to read by encouraging them to make meaning from the different kinds of signs and symbols which surround them in their everyday lives. Here are some suggestions for follow-up activities which extend the ideas introduced in the book.

Pages 2/3 Children could cut out examples of road, rail, land, sea and air transport from old newspapers, magazines and travel brochures. What messages, such as brand names, company logos, advertisements, security protection stickers, destination information, can they find? The children could make a collage to display all the different messages.

Pages 4/5 If it is possible, take the children on a bus ride around the local area. How do the children know where to stand to wait for the bus? How do they know which bus to catch? How do they signal to the driver to stop at the next bus stop? Look at the messages on the inside of the bus, such as signs giving information and warning notices. What are the driver and conductor (if there is one) wearing to show they are members of the bus crew? How many different messages can the children see on their tickets or travel passes?

Pages 6/7 Carry out a survey of the cars in the school car park. What messages, such as, disabled driver, baby on board, member of a breakdown service, member of a leisure organisation, can the children find? Group the cars by age or by make and record the findings in a bar chart.

Pages 8/9 Ask the children to think up features they would include on the dashboard of an imaginary car, for example an ejector seat or ice-cream dispenser. Help the children to make a picture of their customised dashboard, labelling each button, switch and dial. If you live near to an airport, it may be possible to take the children for a visit. Some airports provide resource material specifically for schools. Some children may have travelled in an aeroplane and had the chance to see the cockpit. If so, encourage them to talk about their experiences.

Pages 10/11 Take the children on a short walk around the local area, pointing out the different traffic signs and road markings. Using the Highway Code for reference, show the children examples of some more unusual signs, for example, slippery road surface, low flying aircraft and hump bridge, and ask them to guess what the signs mean. The children could make up their own traffic signs and include them in a large transport mural.

Pages 12/13 If possible, invite a member of the local police force or a representative from the Road Safety Unit or Safety Education Department of your local council to come in and talk to the children about road safety. The children could design their own road safety posters for the school and they could practise the Green Cross Code in the playground.

Pages 14/15 Make a collection of pictures to show how lights are used in transport, for example, Catseyes in the centre of roads, filter arrows as part of a set of traffic lights, indicator lights on vehicles and flashing Belisha beacons at pedestrian crossings.

Pages 16/17 Experiment with musical instruments to make different transport sounds, for example, a ship's foghorn, an ambulance siren, a station tannoy and a car alarm. The children could make up a class story incorporating the different transport sounds.

Pages 18/19 Take the children on a short walk around the local area to investigate how people use their arms to signal to each other, for example, a lollipop person stopping the traffic, a person hailing a taxi, a cyclist making a turn and a policewoman directing the traffic. Back in the classroom, the children could take turns to mime the actions of the people they've seen for everyone else to guess.

Pages 20/21 Set up a classroom railway station with advertising posters and a timetable for 'trains' running between the classroom and the school entrance, calling at stops such as the kitchen and the hall. The children could design their own logo for the station and make their own train tickets. Encourage the children to take part in role-play activities, taking it in turns to be passengers, the driver, the ticket inspector, the station manager and the guard.

Pages 22/23 Collect examples of different maps for the children to look at. Use the maps to talk about map-making, drawing to scale, the points of a compass and the symbols used to indicate the different features of an area covered by a map. The children could draw a simple map of their classroom with symbols to show where things are.

SWAN AIR